Phil Wickham Music
2888 Loker Ave E, Suite 110
Carlsbad CA 92010

Printed in the United States of America.

First edition: 2024

ISBN: 979-8-218-42265-3

Publisher's Cataloging-in-Publication data
Names: Wickham, Phil (Musician), author. I Horning, Benji, author.
Title: I Believe • Devotional / by Phil Wickham; with Benji Horning.
Description: Carlsbad, CA: Phil Wickham Music, 2024.
Identifiers: ISBN: 979-8-218-42265-3
Subjects: LCSH Devotional calendars. I Prayer-Christianity-Meditations. I Christian life-Prayers and devotions. I Faith-Prayers and devotions. I RELIGION / Christian Living / Devotional

14 DAYS TO LIVING A LIFE OF GREATER FAITH

I Believe

DEVOTIONAL

PHIL WICKHAM

with BENJI HORNING

INTRODUCTION

Over the past few years, the world and the Church have been stretched in unimaginable ways. Life that used to feel stable, predictable, and safe has been challenged. This album was birthed out of a deep desire for all of us to be drawn back to the most fundamental elements of our faith. We belong to a Kingdom that will never be shaken, and we follow a crucified and resurrected Savior who is now and forever on the throne. What a reason to worship! We must return to pursuing the One who has always pursued us. These songs were written to boldly proclaim who our God truly is, and to give new lyrics and melodies for us to respond to Him.

As I reflect on this past season, the moments that ignited my heart with renewal and passion were times when I would see people unapologetically profess their hope and faith in Jesus. When it was clear that their belief in God was not something hidden but boldly lived out and professed. In his letter to the church in Rome, the Apostle Paul exhorts them: "I am not ashamed of the gospel, because it is the power of God that brings salvation to everyone who believes" (Romans 1:16 NIV).

The Early Church flourished in a time of heavy persecution, extreme uncertainty, and profound adversity because there was something deeper that drove them past their fear to a place of unflinching passion and devotion to Jesus.

My friends, we need Jesus. This may not sound like a new or novel idea, and it's not supposed to, but this is the very framework of our entire reality. This is the foundation of all our hope and the source of our strength. The culture we are surrounded by has been loudly presenting its own version of solutions and functional saviors, and in the past few years, all of those have been shaken. A.W. Tozer once wrote,

"The burden borne by mankind is a heavy and a crushing thing...

God is so vastly wonderful,

so utterly and completely delightful that He can, without anything other than Himself, meet and overflow the deepest demands of our total nature."

There is only One who is our Cornerstone, the Beginning and End, the Name that is above every other name. Imagine what will happen when we all, His Church, start walking in faith, filled with the Holy Spirit, motivated to love... The world will never be the same, and the desperate longings of all our hearts will finally be satisfied in Him. Over the next 14 days, I hope your faith will be strengthened, your heart captivated, and your soul awakened to the reality of King Jesus! So may we all lay our crowns before Him and shout for all of eternity, "I Believe!"

Key Questions:

1. What areas in your life have you placed your trust in things or people other than Jesus?

2. What does it look like to turn to Him again as your "first love"?

3. What are some intentional habits and patterns you can start to practice to help you put Jesus first again?

Key Bible Verses to Meditate On:

Mark 12:30 (NIV): Love the Lord your God with all your heart and with all your soul and with all your mind and with all your strength.

Revelation 2:4-5 (NIV): You have forsaken the love you had at first. Consider how far you have fallen! Repent, and do the things you did at first.

THIS IS OUR GOD

01

In 2013, I lost my voice. The doctors told me I had a hemorrhaging polyp on my vocal cord, and it required surgery. I met with the surgeon, and she revealed what I was deeply fearful of. She told me that there was a good chance that my voice would never be the same, and I had to prepare myself for that possibility. I was then given strict orders to not sing or talk for the next month. In the silence that followed, I felt all the feelings you might expect... worry, fear, frustration. But what I didn't expect was the feeling that seemed to rise above all the others. As I searched my heart, I realized that without my voice, I felt worthless. My career as a singer is what I had built my identity on. It was how I measured my value as a person. Without it, I didn't know who I was.

Because of the surgery, I had to cancel over fifty events! One of those was a conference called Catalyst West, and they had asked if I would write a few words that could be read aloud from the stage. I was moved by their request. As I sat down to write, I got another text from my main contact at the conference. He said, "I wanted to let you know, that the theme for the conference this year is 'IDENTITY'."

The moment I read that word, the room changed. I felt the weight of God's presence in a way I had only experienced a few times in my life. I was undone. Tears filled my eyes. I didn't want to speak or even move. And then a question filled my soul:

"WHO AM I?"
It was as if I could almost hear Him.

"WHO AM I?"
The question continued to ring in my mind...

In the weight and silence of that moment, my heart replied, "You are my Father."

"AND WHAT DOES THAT MAKE YOU?" The next question rang.

It makes me YOUR CHILD.

5

As my heart said those words, everything changed. Never in my life was I so aware of God's love. His heart for me! For us! It was the greatest spiritual shift in my life since becoming a Christian. The God who created the universe met me in the back room of my house to remind me that I am His child… This means He has good plans for me. He's watching out for me. Before any other identity I carry, I am FIRST, His son! That truth turned my depression into joy, my questions into praise, and my frustration into hope. My prayer changed from "God Help me" to an honest "God I can't wait to see what You have next."

Praise God the surgery went miraculously well, and I was back singing in less than half the time the doctors told me I would be! While it felt amazing to sing again, I was far more thankful for the way God met me in the silence. He showed me who I am by revealing to me who He is!

The author Richard Foster says that in silence there is the potential to "create the emotional and spiritual space which allows Christ to construct the inner sanctuary in the heart."

I took the time to tell this story because it's the very reason why I wrote the song "This Is Our God" and why I made it the first song on the album. True worship—praise, trust, faith, and hope in Jesus—does not come from us being more spiritual or trying harder. It comes from our hearts responding to God as He reveals Himself to us. The more we seek Him, the more we find Him. And the more we find, the greater our response. I find that, over and over again, I forget how great He is. I have learned that I have to intentionally remind myself of His love, grace, power, and promises. That's why this song, and the whole album, begins with the word "*REMEMBER*"! So...

Let us remember all that He has done!
Let us remember the Cross and the
empty grave!
Let us remember how He pulled us out
of the prisons of our sin and shame and
redeemed us into His Kingdom! Our
identity, life, and joy is found in Him and
Him alone!
He is faithful, even when we are faithless!
He is the same, yesterday, today
and forever!

He is the King over all Kings!
He is our Present Father!
He is the Creator of all!
He is the Spotless Lamb!
He is Jesus!

THIS IS OUR GOD!

Key Questions:

1. What areas of your life might be competing for your deepest identity?

2. What does it really mean for you to see yourself as an adopted son or daughter of God?

3. What would it look like for you to intentionally "remember" what your Heavenly Father has done in your life?

Key Bible Verses to Meditate On:

John 15:5 (ESV): I am the vine; you are the branches. Whoever abides in me and I in him, he it is that bears much fruit, for apart from me you can do nothing.

Ephesians 1:4–5 (NIV): For he chose us in him before the creation of the world to be holy and blameless in his sight. In love he predestined us for adoption to sonship through Jesus Christ, in accordance with his pleasure and will

This Is Our God

(based on the recording by Phil Wickham)

Words and Music by
**Phil Wickham, Steven Furtick,
Brandon Lake and Pat Barrett**

INTRO

VERSE 1

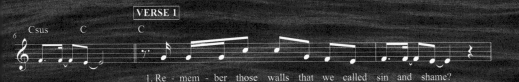

1. Re - mem - ber those walls that we called sin and shame?

They were like pris - ons that we could - n't es - cape. But He came and He died and He rose;

those walls are rub - ble now.

Re - mem - ber those gi - ants we called death and grave?

They were like moun - tains that stood in our way. But He came and He died and He rose;

those gi - ants are dead now. This is our

I BELIEVE

02

In February of 2022, I was invited to the Grammys because my song, "Hymn Of Heaven", was up for an award for "Christian Song Of The Year". It was the first time I had ever been nominated! I was looking forward to the event, but honestly, I was way more excited for an excuse to have a weekend away with my wife, Mallory. After a few smaller pre-event gatherings, the time came for the actual televised Grammy broadcast, and I didn't know what to expect. As a musician and a music fan, I walked in excited to see the show. This was supposed to be the top-tier event with the best of the best of the music industry in attendance.

As the night went on, however, I couldn't help but feel a growing heaviness in my heart. In the midst of all this talent and creativity, there was an absence of acknowledging the Creator behind it all. Greater than any other time in my life, my heart broke for anyone who doesn't know Jesus! I walked in ready to see a show. I walked out wanting to shout the name of Jesus from the rooftops! I knew in my heart I needed a song that would say all that I was feeling.

The next day I wrote the song "I Believe". All I wanted to do was boast in Jesus! I'm so proud of Him! I'm proud of who He is, of what He did, and all that He stands for! It doesn't take much to realize the world is searching for hope, for truth, and for purpose. I believe with all my heart that all those things and more can be found in the person of Jesus Christ. The world is desperate for a group of people armed with love, humility, grace, and the power of the Holy Spirit to stand and say, "This is who Jesus is! This is why I follow Him! And this is why you should too!"

The biblical idea of "belief" does not stop with our minds. It must move us to action and trust. On one occasion, Jesus spoke to a man deep in despair saying in Mark 5:36 (NIV), "Don't be afraid; just believe!" Belief in the original language of the New Testament (*pisteuō*, in Greek) was so much more than intellectual agreement or an elite spiritual status. It meant DEEP TRUST. Imagine a bridge. True "belief" in that bridge is not just acknowledging that it exists, but it is taking steps of faith to walk across. True belief in Jesus is the same. We must place the full weight of our life upon Him! This is why this song calls the Church to declare BOLDLY…

No, I'll never be ashamed
Of the gospel of Jesus Christ
How could I ever walk away
From the One who saved my life?

It's time to stop putting our belief in human achievement, social status, worldly pleasure, and hollow power. We must place the full weight of our life on the One who is worthy of our song, our life, our deep trust—our BELIEF!

Key Questions:

1. Was there a time in your life when you realized what you were chasing after didn't fully satisfy?

2. How does what and who you believe in affect your everyday life?

3. What is something that you have been so excited about that you just had to tell someone? Pray that the Holy Spirit would ignite that kind of fresh passion for the Gospel in your heart again!

4. What are some ways that the reality of who Christ is could cultivate renewed joy, wonder, and praise in the daily, ordinary rhythms of your life?

Key Bible Verses to Meditate On:

John 4:13–14 (NIV): Jesus answered, "Everyone who drinks this water will be thirsty again, but whoever drinks the water I give them will never thirst. Indeed, the water I give them will become in them a spring of water welling up to eternal life."

Romans 1:16 (NIV): For I am not ashamed of the gospel, because it is the power of God that brings salvation to everyone who believes.

I Believe

(based on the recording by Phil Wickham)

Words and Music by
**Chris Davenport, Jonathan Smith
and Phil Wickham**

INTRO **VERSE 1**

1. I be - lieve there is one sal - va - tion, one door - way that leads to life. One re - demp - tion, one con - fes - sion, I be - lieve in the name of Je - sus Christ.

VERSE 2

2. I be - lieve in the cru - ci - fix - ion. By His blood, I have been set free. I be - lieve in the res - ur - rec - tion. Hal - le - lu - jah, His

CHORUS 1a

life is death's de - feat. All praise to God, the Fa - ther, all praise to Christ, the Son. All praise to the Ho - ly Spir - it, our God has

Sunday Is Coming

03

The day Jesus died is considered by many to be the darkest day in the history of the world. Even Jesus, in the moment He was arrested, said, "But this is your hour—when darkness reigns" (Luke 22:53 NIV). So isn't it interesting that billions of people around the world now know this day as GOOD FRIDAY? How can that be? How can we call the day, when a loving God was crushed by the ones He loved, "good"?

John 19:30 (NIV) reads, "Jesus said, 'It is finished.' With that, he bowed his head and gave up his spirit." The last words of Jesus proclaimed that His mission was accomplished! All the weight and guilt of sin came head-to-head with the spotless Lamb of God, and in that moment, all sin—past, present, and future—finally was atoned for!

Isaiah 53:5 (NKJV) says, "By His stripes we are healed." His pain was our healing. His blood our ransom. Our Rescuer, at the cost of His own life, had finally made a path of redemption for all who would believe.

After the horror of the Crucifixion had come to a holy hush, the story enters a long silence. Can you imagine the devastation and confusion that His disciples were crushed by?

The Saturday following Good Friday has been called "Holy Saturday" by the Church for hundreds of years. The beauty of this day is that it very much represents the current state in which we all find ourselves. We are waiting, trusting, hoping that Sunday is coming. We live in what theologians call the "now and not yet." On one hand "it is finished!" And on the other hand, we are waiting for the full effect of the Resurrection. Holy Saturday reminds us that it's only a matter of time... Take heart... Sunday is coming!

There's a hinge point in this song where everything changes....

The women came before the dawn
To find that stone already gone
When they looked inside, the angel said
"Why are you looking for the living among the dead?"

He's alive!
He's alive!
Hallelujah, He's alive!

In Jesus, no matter what we are facing, we can rest assured that for those who follow Him, resurrection is always coming! You see, the Resurrection is a historical event, but it is so much more than just that. Jesus says in John 11:25 (NIV), "I AM the resurrection and the life!" Resurrection is a person! Resurrection is Jesus! Where there is Jesus, there is always everlasting life!

My prayer is that the Good News that Sunday is coming would not be something reserved once a year for Easter, but something that permeates every fiber of your being, every second of your day, every longing of your heart! Remember the promise that "The Spirit of him who raised Jesus from the dead is living in you" (Romans 8:11 NIV).

HE IS ALIVE!
And SO ARE WE!

Key Questions:

1. When Jesus says, "It is finished" on Good Friday, what does that mean for you? How does the peace and assurance of His sacrifice shape your life?

2. Can you think of a season of your life that feels like Holy Saturday? Maybe you're in one right now? What does it look like to make space for the waiting and longing for the renewal of all things? How can this help you understand Jesus' nearness to you in your own longing and waiting?

3. How have you let the Resurrection change your life? How can the Resurrection not just be a once-a-year event but a daily reality that you get to live in?

4. What does it mean that "The Spirit of God, who raised Jesus from the dead, lives in you!" (Romans 8:11)? How does this change how you can live TODAY?

Key Bible Verses to Meditate On:

John 19:30 (NIV): When he had received the drink, Jesus said, "It is finished." With that, he bowed his head and gave up his spirit.

1 Corinthians 15:55–57 (NIV):
"Where, O death, is your victory? Where, O death, is your sting?"
The sting of death is sin, and the power of sin is the law. But thanks be to God! He gives us the victory through our Lord Jesus Christ.

Isaiah 25:8–9 (NIV):
He will swallow up death forever. The Sovereign Lord will wipe away the tears from all faces; he will remove his people's disgrace from all the earth. The Lord has spoken. In that day they will say, "Surely this is our God."

Sunday Is Coming

(based on the recording by Phil Wickham)

Words and Music by
Phil Wickham, Jonathan Smith,
Steven Furtick and Adrian Disch

VERSE 1

1. A great light dawns in Gal - i - lee. Some say, "mad man," some say, "king."

Won - der - work - ing re - bel priest, Je - sus Christ the Naz - a - rene.

He knew well what it would take to free us all from sin and grave.

per - fect man would have to die, and on - ly He could pay that price. Fri-

CHORUS

day's good 'cause Sun - day is com - ing. Don't lose hope, 'cause Sun - day is com - ing.

Dev - il, you're done. You bet - ter start run - ning. Fri-

VERSE 2

day's good 'cause Sun - day is com - ing. 2. So He let those sol - diers take Him in

as His friend be - trayed Him with a kiss. There be - fore the mock - ing crowd

like a lamb to the slaugh - ter, did - n't make a sound. Then He car-

CCLI Song # 7213928

CREATOR

04

My six-year-old son, Henry, loves talking about space. Lately, most nights, as I'm helping him get ready for bed, he asks if there's anything new astronauts have found out about space since we talked about it the day before. I always smile at how cute this question is, but I also feel a little spark of excitement in my own chest. Because you know what? I love talking about space too.

We lay side by side and Google facts about stars and black holes. I try to explain what a light year is. His little six-year-old eyes get so wide when I try to help him understand how small we are compared to the sun, and how small the sun is compared to other stars. How there are billions of stars in our galaxy and countless galaxies spinning outside of our own.

What I love the most about our space conversations is that they inevitably lead back to God.

Henry and I talk about how, in the Bible, the first thing we find out about God is that He is a CREATOR. He imagined and spoke the universe into existence. The laws of nature and physics were literally written by His own hand. He spoke "light" and the entire universe burst into existence. He spoke "life" and everything that lives and breathes came into being. It's incredible! And then we talk about what God made last... Something truly beautiful and unique, made in His own likeness and after His image. Something, or someone rather, God could share the world with. And what was this crown jewel of creation? It was us. Humanity. He created us to know Him and be known by Him. To love Him and be loved by Him. He also created us with an incredible attribute— the ability to trust.

From the very beginning, humanity has been given the choice whether to trust God's definition of what is good and what is bad, or to go off on our own and define those things for ourselves. Eventually, the first man and woman chose not to trust, and every human since has followed the path they walked. The problem with this is that man was made to thrive in God's definition of life and goodness. Just as our lungs were made to breathe oxygen, our souls were made to live in God's presence. To thrive in His goodness and order.

In Genesis 3, humanity became lost. The more we tried to save ourselves, the further away from our original home we fell. We needed a Savior. Someone who could make right what went wrong in the Garden all those years ago. Someone who could bridge the gap between heaven and earth. Opening a door. Making a way. Pulling all who were willing from darkness to light. In Genesis chapter 3, not only do we see the devastation of sin set in motion, but we also have the very first prophetic promise that someday, a rescuer would come. While God is cursing the serpent, he says in Genesis 3:15 (NIV): "He will crush your head, and you will strike his heel." In speaking of the offspring of the woman, we are told that, somehow, all that went wrong in creation would be set right by this "Serpent Crusher" but that He, Himself, would be given a fatal blow as well.

So, when the fullness of time came, the Creator stepped into His own creation to save the ones He loved. He came to bring back to humanity what was stolen by our own rebellion. It was a beautiful and powerful act of love and humility. The Creator wasn't bringing humanity back to the Garden of Eden… He was bringing the Garden into the hearts of Humanity! Every soul that allows Him access becomes a place where heaven and earth meet.

The same voice that said "let there be light" and the universe was formed, was now saying "let there be light" and the hearts of men began to burn again. The same breath that animated every living thing was breathing new life into humanity. The restoration had begun. The ultimate act of creation came as the debt of sin that humanity racked up was fully paid for on the cross. We have been redeemed and set free by His precious blood. In His death, we have been given eternal life!

The last page of the Bible ends with this remarkable declaration:

"He who was seated on the throne said, 'I am making everything new!' (Revelation 21:5 NIV).

God, the Creator, has not and will never stop creating! There is no area of your life beyond His redemptive, creative power. No soul that He cannot breathe new life into! From the opening pages of Scripture to the very end, we are given the same invitation...

Praise Him who stepped into what He made
Paid our debt and pulled us from the grave
Every heart He set free
Every soul that's been redeemed
Lift your voice and worship your Creator!

Key Questions:

1. Why do you think it's so important that the Bible would start and end with the attribute of God being the Creator?

2. How does God's creative and redemptive ability speak hope into your own life? What circumstance do you need to invite the Creator into?

3. How can you spend some intentional time outside today or this week to take notice of all that God has made? What does it look like to be in awe of the order, intricacy, and beauty in creation that was made for our delight and His glory?

Key Bible Verses to Meditate On:

Genesis 1:1–3 (NIV): In the beginning God created the heavens and the earth. Now the earth was formless and empty, darkness was over the surface of the deep, and the Spirit of God was hovering over the waters. And God said, "Let there be light," and there was light.

Romans 1:20 (NIV): For since the creation of the world God's invisible qualities—his eternal power and divine nature—have been clearly seen, being understood from what has been made, so that people are without excuse.

Psalm 8:3–4 (NIV):
When I consider your heavens,
the work of your fingers,
the moon and the stars,
which you have set in place,
what is mankind that you are mindful of them,
human beings that you care for them?

Read and meditate on all of Psalm 104

Creator

(based on recording by Phil Wickham)

Words and Music by
**Phil Wickham, Bryan Fowler
and Kristyn Getty**

VERSE 1, 2 & 3

1. Praise Him all you crea - tures great and small.
2. Praise Him gleam - ing moon and burn - ing sun.
3. Praise Him who stepped in - to what He made,

Praise Him sum - mer, win - ter, spring and fall. Howl - ing wind, rush - ing streams, roll - ing
Praise Him all you spin - ning spheres a - bove. Shin - ing stars, gold - en beams, choir
paid our debt and pulled us from the grave. Ev - 'ry heart He set free, ev - 'ry

hills and crash - ing seas, lift your voice and wor - ship your Cre - at
made of gal - ax - ies, lift your voice and wor - ship your Cre - at
soul that's been re - deemed, lift your voice and wor - ship your Cre - at

CHORUS

or.
or.
or.

Ho - ly. You are ho - ly. Earth and heav - en sing for -

ev - er. Ho - ly, You are ho - ly. All cre - a - tion praise Cre - at - or,

PRAISE THE LORD

05

LET EVERYTHING WITHIN ME PRAISE THE LORD

Praise Him because He's amazing!
Take a walk in the morning. Hear the birds sing. Feel the sun on your skin. Notice the details. He's in them all. And they're all singing "Praise the Lord" in their own unique way.

Take a walk at night. Look at the moon and the stars. Consider their distance and the vastness of it all. If you could see a million galaxies, each with a billion stars, you still wouldn't be scratching the surface of what's out there. He holds it all together, and it's all singing "Praise the Lord" in its own unique way.

Praise Him for what He has done!
He died for us so that we could live. He bled for us so our debt could be paid. He was forsaken so we could be forgiven. He was rejected so we could be adopted into the family of the King of Kings. We stand in the victory that He has won. The story did not end on the cross, but it continues today and forevermore because HE IS ALIVE! The grave where He once lay is empty. Not because His body was moved, but because HE WALKED OUT OF IT! Death has lost its grip on us. Hell has no power over us. We are sons and daughters of the Most High because of the Cross and the empty grave.

PRAISE HIM

with all that is within you!

Let your life be a response to who He is and what He has done!

Let your desires be praise to Him! If they're not, then redirect them. Let your dreams be praise to Him–your ambitions, passions, creativity, and motivations. Let them be a song of praise to God.

Let your thoughts be praise to Him! If they're not, then redirect them. Think on things that bring Him glory and please His heart. The way you think about others and yourself. The way you think about material things and finances.

St. Augustine, in his book *Confessions*, wrote, "You have made us for yourself, O Lord, and our hearts are restless until they rest in You."

Let your life be praise to God! Your relationships, obedience, faith, and trust. The way you act and the way you react to others. In your frustrations and fears. In your joys and laughter. In your highs and lows.

In light of all that He is, all that He's done, all that He's promised, all that He's doing. Praise the Lord!

Key Questions:

1. Where has your attention and adoration—which was ultimately made to be directed at God—been directed this week?

2. What does it mean to praise God with your life and not just with song? What do you sense the Holy Spirit asking you to do to move more fully toward a life that is worship to Jesus?

3. How can you practically adjust your habits and priorities to give God praise? Worship on your commute? Prioritize gathering on Sundays with other believers? Start and end your day with gratitude?

Key Bible Verses to Meditate On:

Psalm 148:1–5 (NIV):
Praise the Lord from the heavens;
praise him in the heights above.
Praise him, all his angels;
praise him, all his heavenly hosts.
Praise him, sun and moon;
praise him, all you shining stars.
Praise him, you highest heavens
and you waters above the skies.
Let them praise the name of the Lord.

Romans 12:1–2 (NIV): Therefore, I urge you, brothers and sisters, in view of God's mercy, to offer your bodies as a living sacrifice, holy and pleasing to God—this is your true and proper worship. Do not conform to the pattern of this world, but be transformed by the renewing of your mind. Then you will be able to test and approve what God's will is—his good, pleasing and perfect will.

Colossians 3:17 (NIV): And whatever you do, whether in word or deed, do it all in the name of the Lord Jesus, giving thanks to God the Father through him.

Praise The Lord

(based on the recording by Phil Wickham)

Words and Music by
**Brandon Lake, Jonathan Smith,
Mia Fieldes, Phil Wickham
and Steven Furtick**

THE JESUS WAY

06

It took me three years to finish writing "The Jesus Way".

All the verse lyrics came to me in a single instance of pen to paper during a season of frustration and confusion. I was asking God where I fit into it all, and He answered me. This is what was written:

"If you curse me I will bless you
If you hurt me, I will forgive
And if you hate me, I will love you
I choose THE JESUS WAY

If you're helpless, I will defend you
If you're burdened, I'll share the weight
And if you're hopeless, then let me show you
There's hope in THE JESUS WAY

If you strike me, I will embrace you
If you chain me, I'll sing His praise
and if you kill me, my home is Heaven
For I choose THE JESUS WAY!"

The words came out so fast that I honestly had to reread what I had just written to fully grasp it. As I did, I was moved to tears, overwhelmed by the heart and person of Jesus. How good, patient, loving, and kind He is. I was equally overwhelmed with how often and deeply I fall short of looking and acting like Him. God was simultaneously blowing my mind with His character and breaking my heart with the reality of my need for a Savior.

At first, I just saw the words on the page as a sort of prayerful declaration of who He is and who I aim to be. But as the months and years passed, the words didn't get lost in memory. Instead, they grew into a melody that I would often sing to myself. I would hum it in the morning before tackling the day. I would recite it in moments of feeling taken advantage of or tempted to take a less holy path. I used those verses, and the melody that grew around them, to remind my heart of who He is and who I have chosen to be. To preach to my soul what is the Way, the Truth, and the Life!

For a long time, I thought this song was only for me. The idea of releasing and carrying a song that says so decisively and unashamedly that "I choose the Jesus Way" felt daunting to me. I so often decide to choose "The Phil Way" instead, you know? But I couldn't shake the pull inside. I felt that God wanted me to finish the song and give other people the chance to sing along.

So, I set out to write a chorus that would carry the same heart as the verses. It took me months of writing several different choruses and then one finally came flowing out that I wanted to sing over and over:

"I follow Jesus
I follow Jesus
He wore my sin
I'll gladly wear His Name
He is the treasure
He is the answer
I choose the Jesus Way"

I showed the whole song to my good friend and producer Jonathan Smith, and together we wrote a bridge and buttoned the whole thing up. In twenty years of writing songs, I've never had a song personally impact me the way "The Jesus Way" has, and I believe it will continue to for the rest of my life. I have no idea what God has planned for this song, but I am excited to watch His story for it unfold. I hope and pray that this song turns hearts and eyes to Jesus in the same way that it has turned mine to Him.

The Jesus Way was never promised to be easy. But it does promise to be full of meaning and abundant life! You and I were created to know and be known by God. To walk in His presence and His abundant life. Humanity lost its way. The Jesus Way is our roadmap from heaven to find our way back to Him. The more we align ourselves with Him—His way, His truth, and His life—the more we become who we were always meant to be! Peace follows. Joy follows. LIFE follows! May we now and forever declare together that we choose "The Jesus Way!"

Key Questions:

1. What does it mean for you to live the Jesus Way? What areas in your life have you been living according to your own way or the way of the world that you sense the Holy Spirit drawing you back toward Jesus?

2. Have you responded to Jesus' invitation to follow Him? Not just a one-time decision you made a while ago, but one that you choose to make today? What does that practically look like for your life?

3. Is there something radical Jesus is asking you to do? Something to leave? Something to pursue? Something to trust Him with?

Key Bible Verses to Meditate On:

Find some time to read through the entire Sermon on the Mount (Matthew 5-7). Read it slowly, and even if it takes you a few days, take the time to hide it in your heart.

Ephesians 5:1–2 (NIV): Follow God's example, therefore, as dearly loved children [2] and walk in the way of love, just as Christ loved us and gave himself up for us.

John 14:6–7 (NIV): Jesus answered, "I am the way and the truth and the life. No one comes to the Father except through me. [7] If you really know me, you will know my Father as well."

The Jesus Way

(based on the recording by Phil Wickham)

Words and Music by
Phil Wickham and Jonathan Smith

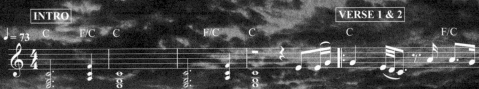

INTRO ♩ = 73

VERSE 1 & 2

1.If you curse me, then I will
(2. If you're) help - less, I will de-

bless you. If you hurt me, I will for - give. And if you
fend you. And if you're burd - ened, I'll share the weight. And if you're

hate me, then I will love you. I choose the Je - sus way.
hope - less, then let me show you there's

CHORUS 1a

2. If you're hope in the Je - sus way. I fol - low Je - sus, I fol - low

Je - sus. He wore my sin, I'll glad - ly wear His name. He is the treas - ure, He is the

WAIT

07

"Do not leave Jerusalem, but WAIT for the gift my Father promised, which you have heard me speak about. For John baptized with water, but in a few days you will be baptized with the Holy Spirit" (Acts 1:4–5 NIV).

The original idea for this song was sent to me by my friend and fellow songwriter, Jacob Sooter. While he was helping produce a live worship album in the UK, the Holy Spirit was moving in a unique and powerful way. One night, conversation was stirring around what God had been up to that day. A seasoned leader in the UK worship movement began to speak about how the Church in Britain has a unique quality to collectively know how to *wait* on the Lord.

He proceeded by saying, "The longer we wait, the more He can do." That comment went with Jacob into the writing room and this song began to take shape.

The reality is that many of us think that in order for God to move, He must be reliant on our influence or gifting to make things happen. This framework is largely shaped by the fast-paced, performance-obsessed, and success-driven culture that we are surrounded by. The Bible, however, actually offers us a counter-narrative. Again and again, Scripture invites us to "wait patiently on the Lord" (Psalm 40:1 NIV).

We must become aware of the seductive nature of the world around us and its demand for us to run faster than what is healthy for our soul or what God has asked of us. For instance…

• Despite access to social media, we seem to be more lonely not less.[1]
• Instead of having more time because of technology, we are more stressed than ever.[2]
• We've never had more Bible study tools available at our fingertips, yet we are finding it harder to find time to sit with Jesus in Scripture.[3]
• Even pastors and church leaders have some of the highest rates of stress and burnout.[4]

There must be a better way… I wonder if this is what Jesus had in mind when He said in Matthew 11:28, "Come to me all you who are weary and heavy burdened, and I will give you rest."

Perhaps what we need is not *more* of something, but *less*. Maybe instead of more striving, we need more surrender. Maybe instead of learning to *do* more, we need to relearn what it means to first just *be* with Him. Maybe we, as His Church, need to learn to *WAIT* on Him again.

---

[1] https://www.health.harvard.edu/blog/is-a-steady-diet-of-social-media-unhealthy-2018122115600

[2] https://time.com/3754781/1965-predictions-computers/

[3] https://research.lifeway.com/2017/07/10/discipling-in-an-age-of-biblical-illiteracy/

[4] https://www.barna.com/research/pastors-well-being/

The prophet Isaiah says…

They who WAIT for the Lord
shall renew their strength;
they shall mount up with wings like
eagles;
they shall run and not be weary;
They shall walk and not faint.
Isaiah 40:31 (ESV)

So how do we respond? What do we do? Maybe the answer is less about our response and more about our posture. Maybe this is less about what we do and more about *how we come* before Him!

Remember friends…
He is strong when we are weak!
He is faithful when we are faithless!
He is at work when we wait!

So, let us
WAIT
on Him!

Key Questions:

1. Are there areas in your life in which you feel you have rushed ahead past the pace or purpose God has called you to? How can you adjust that?

2. What does it look like to take intentional time in your day and week to actually wait on God?

3. What practical steps can you take to create more margin and space to keep in step with and wait on the Spirit?

Key Bible Verses to Meditate On:

2 Peter 3:8–9 (NIV): But do not forget this one thing, dear friends: With the Lord a day is like a thousand years, and a thousand years are like a day. The Lord is not slow in keeping his promise.

Lamentations 3:25–26 (NIV):
The Lord is good to those whose hope is in him,
to the one who seeks him;
it is good to wait quietly
for the salvation of the Lord.

Matthew 11:28-30 (MSG): Are you tired? Worn out? Burned out on religion? Come to me. Get away with me and you'll recover your life. I'll show you how to take a real rest. Walk with me and work with me—watch how I do it. Learn the unforced rhythms of grace. I won't lay anything heavy or ill-fitting on you. Keep company with me and you'll learn to live freely and lightly.

Wait

(based on the recording by Phil Wickham)

Words and Music by
**Chandan Bangar, Jacob Sooter,
Jane Williams, Phil Wickham
and Ran Jackson**

1. Wher - ev - er I go, I'm in Your shad - ow, I'm in Your pres - ence. Up to the heav - ens, un - der the o - cean, I'm in Your pres - ence.
2. There is a still - ness in all the mad - ness here in Your pres - ence. My heart is teth - ered; I wan - na stay here. Oh, I love Your pres - ence.

CHORUS 1

'Cause the long - er I wait the more You can do, and the deep - er I fall in love with You. So I wait, wait for You.

Psalm 23

08

A couple of years ago, while reading my Bible, I came across Psalm 23. Growing up as a son of parents in full-time ministry, this chapter was all too familiar to me. I could probably quote the entire thing from memory since I was five years old. Typically... when I'd come across this Psalm, I would find myself skimming over the verses since I "already knew it."

What should have been a source of transformation and wonder now was predictable. This time, however, I felt the Holy Spirit wake me up to the reality of what I was reading… "The Lord is MY Shepherd"! Something began to move in my heart in a fresh and powerful way! I began to think about the implications of Him truly being MY Shepherd and how that means there is nothing I lack. This beautiful truth changes EVERYTHING!

It changes how I approach my relationships. Instead of needing something from another person, I can come ready to give, because I have all I need in Him.

It changes how I view my circumstances. Instead of me needing to control every outcome, I can release my grip and surrender in peace to the loving will of my Shepherd.

It changes how I view my burdens. Instead of needing to privately shoulder the weight that builds under the stress of life, I can follow His voice to green pastures, quiet waters, and a restored soul.

It changes how I view even the darkness of the valley. Not only is the Shepherd watching over me, He is IN the valley with me. He is walking with me, guarding me, comforting me, as we journey TOGETHER.

Psalm 23 is an invitation into a renewed idea of what it means for Jesus to be your Shepherd. To trust He is leading you and has good plans! That His goodness and mercy are not only present, but they are pursuing you! May you believe and rest in the fact that He is with you even through the darkness of the valley. May you be satisfied in His love and acceptance. May your cup run over at the Table! Let the reality of His Presence set you free from fear, striving, and insecurity!

He is YOUR Shepherd, and you have all you need in Him!

Key Questions:

1. What does it mean that the Lord is YOUR Shepherd? How does that reality bring peace to your heart and mind?

2. When are there moments in the midst of your own valleys that you can see God's presence near to you?

3. At the end of Psalm 23, it gives us a picture of a banquet where our cups are running over and His goodness and mercy are pursuing us for all of eternity. How does this stir up your hope? How can this give you strength for the journey?

Key Bible Verses to Meditate On:

Psalm 23:1–6 (NIV):
The Lord is my shepherd, I lack nothing.
He makes me lie down in green pastures,
he leads me beside quiet waters,
he refreshes my soul.
He guides me along the right paths
for his name's sake.
Even though I walk
through the darkest valley,
I will fear no evil,
for you are with me;
your rod and your staff,
they comfort me.
You prepare a table before me
in the presence of my enemies.
You anoint my head with oil;
my cup overflows.
Surely your goodness and love will follow me
all the days of my life,
and I will dwell in the house of the Lord
forever.

Psalm 23

(based on the recording by Phil Wickham, feat. Tiffany Hudson)

Words and Music by
Phil Wickham

INTRO

♩ = 65

D   Bm7   Asus   D/F♯   G2   Bm7   Asus

VERSE 1

D   Bm7   Asus   D/F♯

1. The Lord is my shep-herd; there's noth-ing I need. You lead me to the

G2(no3)   Bm7   Asus   A

saf-est plac-es, You lead me to the saf-est plac-es.

D   Bm7   Asus   D/F♯

To walk in the mead-ow and lie by the stream, You meet me in the

G2(no3)   Bm7   Asus   A(4)

qui-et plac-es. You meet me in the qui-et plac-es. Your good-

CHORUS 1

G   D   Asus   Bm7   G   D

ness and Your mer-cy will fol-low me all the days of my life, all the days

Asus   G   D   Asus   Bm7

of my life. And I'll dwell in Your house for e-ter-ni-ty. I'll be there by Your

ISN'T HE GOOD

09

The Hebrew word for "good" is *"Tov"* (pronounced "tove"). This simple word is packed with significance and is used hundreds of times throughout the Old Testament. On the very first page of the Bible, we see this concept introduced when God pronounces a blessing over His creation seven times. He declares everything *"Tov"* at the end of each poetic refrain. The only break from this pattern was after He created humanity in His image. Looking over Adam and Eve, instead of just saying this is *"Tov,"* He said this is *"Tov Tov."* This double use of the word is a Jewish way to say this is "VERY GOOD!" Humanity is His crown jewel in all of creation!

Not only was God the one who pronounced goodness over His creation, but He was also the one who defined for Adam and Eve what was good and what was not. When sin enters the story in Genesis 3, it arrives because the first humans stopped trusting God's definition of good and evil. Instead, they attempted to define it on their own terms. All of humanity has followed this pattern, including you and me.

What's important to remember is that God gets to define what is "good" because He is the very essence of the word! In Mark 10:18 (NIV),

Jesus himself comments on this when He is confronted with a religious question and responds, "No one is good—except God alone." Jesus deflects the compliment and draws the listener's attention to the goodness of His Father!

This song is a declaration of the truth that has been woven throughout the entire biblical story that God is GOOD! What He creates and how He orders His creation is GOOD! And, by His grace, He sustains and finishes what is GOOD! Consider how the apostle Paul writes, "And I am sure of this, that he who began a GOOD work in you will bring it to completion at the day of Jesus Christ" (Philippians 1:6 ESV).

The truth is, we live in a time in history when there is a constant war that's raging about the definition of what is true, beautiful, and good. When the pressure of the cultural voices around us feels disorienting and discouraging, remember that…

God is the epitome of good!
What He creates is good!
How He has ordered His creation is good!
And what He is moving His creation toward is
wrapped up in His good and redemptive plan!

This is why the refrain at the end of this chorus is more than a question… it is a call to action! May we boldly declare that God and God alone is worthy of our praise. He is good! He is great! He is faithful!

And He is forever and always worthy!

Key Questions:

1. What good things has God done in your life? How have you seen His faithful hand at work?

2. In what areas of your life can you trust that God has good plans and that the good things He began, He will carry to completion?

3. What can it look like this week to direct great passion and devotion toward declaring the goodness of our God?

Key Bible Verses to Meditate On:

Psalm 27:13 (NIV):
I remain confident of this:
I will see the goodness of the Lord
in the land of the living.

Nahum 1:7 (NIV):
The Lord is good,
a refuge in times of trouble.
He cares for those who trust in him.

Psalm 34:8 (NIV):
Taste and see that the Lord is good;
blessed is the one who takes refuge in him.

Isn't He Good

(based on the recording by Phil Wickham)

Words and Music by
**Brandon Lake, Phil Wickham,
Ricky Jackson and Steven Furtick**

100%

10

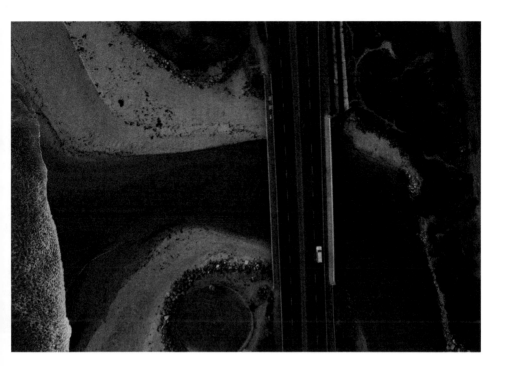

The opening line of this verse says:

I'm a little scared to sing this song / Cause I know it's coming with a cost / But You said I got to die to live / So God I'm picking up my cross"

I remember wrestling through these lyrics as I considered the invitation that Jesus gave again and again throughout the Gospels when He says, "If anyone wants to follow after me, let him deny himself, take up his cross, and follow me" (Matthew 16:24 CSB).

The reality is that Jesus never said this would be easy. In fact, he prepared His disciples for the opposite in Luke 14:33 (ESV) with these sobering words, "So therefore, any one of you who does not renounce all that he has cannot be my disciple." What a radical invitation!

Every follower of Jesus is invited down a narrow but beautiful road. Many will prefer the easy way, but Jesus begins to unpack the secret for His followers when He says in Matthew 7 that this seemingly unattractive path of sacrifice actually leads to life! Jesus is passionate about providing abundant life to His children! In one conversation, He tells His disciples that "The thief comes only to steal and kill and destroy; I have come that they may have life, and have it to the full" (John 10:10 NIV).

But here is the great paradox of the Gospel...

Matthew 10:39 (NIV) says, "Whoever finds their life will lose it, and whoever loses their life for my sake will find it."

If we truly want to follow Jesus with our life, then our life is something we must lose. The Apostle Paul says it like this: "My old self has been crucified with Christ. It is no longer I who live, but Christ lives in me. So I live in this earthly body by trusting in the Son of God, who loved me and gave himself for me" (Galatians 2:20 NLT).

C.S. Lewis once said "The more we let God take us over, the more truly ourselves we become—because He made us. He invented us. He invented all the different people that you and I were intended to be."

What if this great paradox is actually an invitation to great peace and fullness of life?

There is nothing that we can give up to God that He did not first generously give to us, and every time we give up ourselves, we make room for Him to fill us with His abundance! This is why later in the song I wrote:

God, I'll give You anything You ask / Nothing I have

You didn't give me first / And I gladly give it all back

It's like trading in a star to get the universe.

Why is Jesus worthy of giving up everything for? Well, because that is exactly what He did for you, and for me, and for the world He loves so much! We are not asked to do anything that Jesus did not first do for us! I once heard a pastor say, "We cannot call ourselves followers of Jesus and expect an easier life than He had."

We only pick up our cross because Jesus picked up the Cross first.

We only give up our lives because Jesus gave up His life first!

John makes this very clear in his letter to the Church when he wrote, "We love because he first loved us" (1 John 4:19 NIV).

So, when it feels like following Jesus is costing you greatly, remember this promise from Him: "In this world you will have trouble. But take heart! I have overcome the world" (John 16:33 NIV).

The greatest response we can have to the radical love of Jesus giving up His life and picking up His cross is to worship Him in the same manner. This cannot just be with music and song but must be with our whole life! May we not settle for giving Jesus some of us, or even most of us, may we relentlessly follow Him in such a way that He may have ALL of us!

Key Questions:

1. What areas in your life have you been holding back from God? What fear do you have in fully surrendering to God?

2. What would it look like for you to spend time meditating on the enormity of the sacrifice that Jesus made for you? How can this propel you to give more of yourself?

3. Who in your life can you include on this journey of giving over to God your whole life?

Key Bible Verses to Meditate On:

2 Corinthians 5:15 (NIV): He died for all, that those who live should no longer live for themselves but for him who died for them and was raised again.

Mark 8:34–36 (NIV): Then he called the crowd to him along with his disciples and said: "Whoever wants to be my disciple must deny themselves and take up their cross and follow me. For whoever wants to save their life will lose it, but whoever loses their life for me and for the gospel will save it. What good is it for someone to gain the whole world, yet forfeit their soul?"

Luke 14:27-30, 33 (CSB): "Whoever does not bear his own cross and come after me cannot be my disciple. For which of you, wanting to build a tower, doesn't first sit down and calculate the cost to see if he has enough to complete it? Otherwise, after he has laid the foundation and cannot finish it, all the onlookers will begin to ridicule him, saying, 'This man started to build and wasn't able to finish'... In the same way, therefore, every one of you who does not renounce all his possessions cannot be my disciple."

100%

(based on the recording by Phil Wickham)

Words and Music by
**Phil Wickham, Evan Wickham
and Jonathan Smith**

♩ = 67 **VERSE 1**

D2(no3)

1. I'm a lit - tle scared to sing this song, 'cause I know it's com - ing with a cost.

A

But You said I got to die to live, so God I'm pick - ing up my cross.

D2(no3)

'Cause I've tast - ed what the world gives, the things they say that mat - ter most,

A

and all of it com - pared to You, no, it does - n't e - ven come close.

CHORUS

D2

You can have it all, ev - 'ry sin - gle part. Giv - ing You a hun - dred per - cent of my

A

heart. An - y - thing it costs for ev - 'ry - thing You are. You can have a hun - dred per - cent of my

D2   Esus

heart. All of my life sur - ren - dered, Je - sus, I'm Yours for - ev - er.

Your Name Is Holy

11

This song opens with lyrics declaring that:

There's never been anyone like You God. No one above You. No one beside You.

These lyrics carry special significance for me, but more importantly, special significance in Scripture. The word "Holy" is used over 600 times in the Bible. This word has many layers and dimensions but one of the strongest definitions is to be "set apart," to be totally "other"!

To describe God, the Bible uses hundreds of attributes and adjectives, but it's His "holiness" that stands completely unique above all the others. We know this because, in the Jewish written language, there are no punctuation marks. So, if an author wants to get your attention, he will repeat a word twice. Think of Jesus saying "Truly, truly, I say to you…" It's the author's version of putting something in ALL CAPS or adding multiple exclamation marks. When a Jewish author wants something to go even a step above that, they will repeat it three times! This is so rare that it only happens once in the Old Testament and once in the New Testament, and both times it takes place at the throne of God where angelic creatures shout back and forth to one another that He is

"HOLY, HOLY, HOLY!"

For both the Prophet Isaiah (Isaiah 6:3-4) and the Apostle John (Revelation 4:8), when the curtain was pulled back, and they were given a front-row ticket to the Throne Room of God, they both encountered these winged creatures singing about His holiness! In Isaiah's account, this is so powerful that the very columns of the divine throne room begin to shake! Imagine that. The strongest structural component of Heaven quaking at the sound of God's holiness!

In Revelation, John records that, as "HOLY, HOLY, HOLY" is being proclaimed, the twenty-four Elders who surround the throne have no option but to take the crowns off their own heads and lay them before Him!

God's holiness means that there is no one like Him! He is completely other! There is nothing to compare Him to! There is no equal, nothing similar, nothing close to His strength, His majesty, His glory, His love, His justice, His mercy, His very presence!

Nothing holds more potential for our transformation than the Holy Spirit giving us a glimpse of the radical set apart-ness of our God!

One author puts it this way: "Holiness is the perfection of all [God's] other attributes. His power is holy power, His mercy is holy mercy, His wisdom is holy wisdom. It is His holiness more than any other attribute that makes Him worthy of our praise."[5]

What does this mean for us? What is the appropriate response to the holiness of God? Well, if we take our cues from the books of Revelation and Isaiah, the only adequate response is full, radical, crown-dismounting, earth-shaking WORSHIP!

Worship in light of the holiness of God must be more than a familiar song or tame tradition! God's holiness calls for a burning passion, a surrendered life, arms and eyes lifted up, radical obedience, honest confession, uncompromising trust, and full allegiance to the Name of Jesus! Because…

At the name of Jesus every knee should bow, in heaven and on earth and under the earth, and every tongue acknowledge that Jesus Christ is Lord, to the glory of God the Father.

Philippians 2:10–11 (NIV)

---

[5]Bridges, J. (2016). The pursuit of holiness. NavPress.

Key Questions:

1. In A.W. Tozer's book, *Knowledge of The Holy*, he says that "What comes into our minds when we think about God, is the most important thing about us." What comes to your mind when you think about God? Is it His holiness? How can holiness begin to color how you see every other attribute of God?

2. Does your life reflect the reality that God is holy? What would change in your life if you were to find yourself encountering that same divine throne room of His holy presence?

3. How can you create space in your life to see Jesus high and lifted up through your times of prayer, Scripture reading, and worship?

Key Bible Verses to Meditate On:

Revelation 4:8–11 (NIV): Each of the four living creatures had six wings and was covered with eyes all around, even under its wings. Day and night they never stop saying:

"'Holy, holy, holy
is the Lord God Almighty,'
who was, and is, and is to come."

Whenever the living creatures give glory, honor and thanks to him who sits on the throne and who lives for ever and ever, the twenty-four elders fall down before him who sits on the throne and worship him who lives for ever and ever. They lay their crowns before the throne and say:

"You are worthy, our Lord and God,
to receive glory and honor and power."

Isaiah 6:1–3 (NIV): I saw the Lord, high and exalted, seated on a throne; and the train of his robe filled the temple. Above him were seraphim, each with six wings: With two wings they covered their faces, with two they covered their feet, and with two they were flying. And they were calling to one another:

"Holy, holy, holy is the Lord Almighty;
the whole earth is full of his glory."

Your Name Is Holy

(based on the recording by Phil Wickham)

Words and Music by
**Brian Johnson, Jonathan Smith,
Phil Wickham and Sean Curran**

INTRO

1.There's

VERSE 1

nev - er been an - y - one like You, God.　　　There's

nev - er been an - y - one like You, God.　　No one a - bove You, no one be - side

You, there's nev - er been an - y - one like You, God.　　2.There's

VERSE 2

nev - er been an - y - one like You, God.　　　There's

nev - er been an - y - one like You, God.　　You are the high - est, You are the great-

est, there's nev - er been an - y - one like You, God.

RELATIONSHIP

12

When Jesus came on the scene, the people He preached to were highly religious. The Jewish people built their lives, community, and culture around the Law of Moses. In fact, the spiritual leaders of the Jewish people at the time were so focused on carrying out their interpretation of the Law that they seemed to forget about what the Law was there to do in the first place. When God gave the Law to Moses, it was meant to ultimately lead them back to the heart of the Father.

By the time Jesus showed up, the pursuit of religious excellence had overtaken what should have been most important: justice, mercy, compassion, humility, forgiveness, and ultimately, love of God and neighbor. Jesus showed us these were the things that truly mattered to the Father. To a people who were tirelessly trying to achieve holiness through works and religion and still failing at it, Jesus came to offer Himself as the answer.

Come to me all of you who are weary and burdened down and I will give rest. Take my yoke upon you and learn from me, for I am gentle and humble in heart and I will give you rest. For my yoke is easy and my burden is light.

Matthew 11:28-30 (NIV)

These words must have been like refreshing rain on dry ground for so many hearts who heard them, and these words are just as powerful for us today. How many times, Believer, have you measured your value and standing with God against how "good" of a Christian you've been? How many times have we let guilt and shame keep us from talking to Him because we think we need to live some "holy" days before we do? How many times have we viewed our faith as a checklist to get through rather than a relationship to enjoy?

The older I get, and the more conversations I have, the more I realize that many people have ideas about Jesus and church that have been colored and skewed by things outside of Jesus and the Bible itself. But when I simply talk about Jesus with people, hearts almost always seem to soften. He hated injustice and rebuked hypocrisy. He loved the sinner and embraced the outcast. He could have lived like royalty yet, instead, chose to meet the poor right where they were at. He forgave and healed and set free. He reached out and touched the ones no one else would. He bled and died as an innocent man of His own will so we could have the opportunity to be forgiven and set free from the debt of our own sin. He rose again from the grave and said we can follow Him out of the grave in the same way. He fills us with that same power today to experience the Kingdom of Heaven in the here and now!

He is King. He is Lord. AND He is friend. What a joy it is to know Him!

Thank you, Jesus,

that you call us into relationship with you!

Key Questions:

1. We live in a world that demands performance and achievement to be accepted. Have you ever found yourself trying to perform or work for your Heavenly Father's approval? If so, how?

2. Have you ever found yourself looking down on others or casting judgment on people? How can focusing on God's grace toward you help change how you view others?

3. What does it mean that Jesus calls you friend? How would your relationship with Jesus change if you truly embraced this invitation?

Key Bible Verses to Meditate On:

Mark 2:16–17 (NIV): When the teachers of the law who were Pharisees saw him eating with the sinners and tax collectors, they asked his disciples: "Why does he eat with tax collectors and sinners?" On hearing this, Jesus said to them, "It is not the healthy who need a doctor, but the sick. I have not come to call the righteous, but sinners."

Romans 2:4 (NIV): God's kindness is intended to lead you to repentance.

John 15:15 (NIV): "I no longer call you servants, because a servant does not know his master's business. Instead, I have called you friends, for everything that I learned from my Father I have made known to you."

Relationship

(based on the recording by Phil Wickham)

Words and Music by
**Phil Wickham, Steven Furtick
and Brandon Lake**

INTRO

♩ = 80

1. I know the One who
(2. You met me in the)

VERSE 1 & 2

made the stars. I met Him on the bath-room floor when ev-'ry-thing was
mess I made and told me I was meant for more. You pulled me out of

torn a part. Did-n't know what I was liv-ing for. I al-most gave
my mis-takes and led me through that o-pen door. That's when I woke

1

up. I al-most gave up. 2. You met me in the

2

up. That's when I woke   up, yeah.

CHORUS

My sin is gone and for-giv-en, that shame at the bot-tom of the sea.

You did-n't come for re-li-gion; You want a re-la-tion-ship with me.

CCLI Song # 7220843

BACK TO LIFE

13

Have you ever thought about the fact that the primary way that God chose to reveal Himself to us is through story? The Bible is filled with poems, prayers, sermons, genealogies, and proverbs, but the most common genre of the Scriptures is narrative! I think God chose to do this because He knows us best. He knows that it's through story that we find our greatest meaning and purpose.

One of my favorite stories comes from the dramatic scene in John 11 where Jesus finds Himself at the tomb of His best friend, Lazarus. By the time Jesus got there, Lazarus had been dead for four days. In Jewish tradition, the soul would hover over the body for three days, but on the fourth, there would be no more hope for any reversal of the loss. This little cultural detail sets up the story to show that Jesus is being faced with an impossible situation. Surrounded by weeping family members and friends, the loud and emotional scene comes to a divine pause, and then Jesus calls out…

"'Lazarus, come out!' The dead man came out, his hands and feet wrapped with strips of linen, and a cloth around his face. Jesus said to them, '"Take off the grave clothes and let him go.'"

John 11:43–44 (NIV)

This song carries significance because it reminds us that this story is OUR STORY! This is not just a historical event, which it is, but it's so much more! Apart from Jesus, you and I are without hope, without life, and without promise. But, with Jesus, the One who has called us "friend," no matter how far gone we think we are, no matter how tightly we feel wrapped under the weight of the proverbial grave clothes, we can all still hear the powerful and authoritative voice of Jesus calling out to us "(insert your name here)... COME OUT! Take off the grave clothes and be free!"

I remember when my friend, Brian Johnson, and I were first seeing this song come to life. There was so much excitement in the room as we imagined other believers singing out this core Gospel truth. Because of the Cross and the Resurrection, we can all sing:

No longer I who live, but Christ in me / For I've been born again, my heart is free / The hope of heaven before me, the grave behind / Hallelujah, You brought me back to life

This is the GOOD NEWS that Jesus continues to declare, that IN HIM…

There is no grave that He has not conquered
There is no death that He cannot resurrect
There is no pain that He cannot comfort
There is no sickness that He cannot heal
There is no shame that He cannot cover
There is no bondage that He cannot break

Why?

Because, just like Lazarus… He has called us back to LIFE!

For everyone who would receive Christ's free and complete gift of salvation, this is no longer just *A* story… this is *OUR* story!

Key Questions:

1. Have you heard Jesus call YOUR name out of the grave? If not, take a minute to pray and ask Jesus to become the Lord and Savior of your life. Let His grace pull you from death to life, and confess that by following Him, you are leaving your old "grave clothes" behind.

2. What areas of your life, or your faith, have you given up hope on? How might Jesus invite the hope of His resurrection power to come over you?

3. In the story found in John 11, after Jesus resurrects Lazarus, He invites those watching to unwrap the grave clothes. What would it look like in your own life to join Jesus in helping unwrap those around you from the heavy burden of their previous bondage?

Key Bible Verses to Meditate On:

Read all of John 11

Galatians 2:20 (NIV): I have been crucified with Christ and I no longer live, but Christ lives in me. The life I now live in the body, I live by faith in the Son of God, who loved me and gave himself for me.

Romans 8:11 (NIV): And if the Spirit of him who raised Jesus from the dead is living in you, he who raised Christ from the dead will also give life to your mortal bodies because of his Spirit who lives in you.

Back To Life

(based on the recording by Bethel Music & Zahriya Zachary)

Words and Music by
**Brian Johnson, Phil Wickham,
Chris Davenport, Reuben Morgan,
Ben Fielding and Zahriya Zachary**

CHORUS

No long - er I who live, but Christ in me for I've been

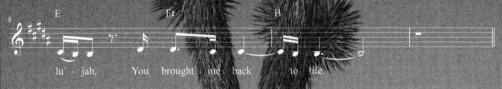

born a - gain, my heart is free. The hope of heav - en be - fore me, the grave be - hind. Hal - le -

lu - jah, You brought me back to life.

VERSE 1 & 2

1. I won't for - get the mo - ment I heard You call my name
2. Where there was dead re - li - gion, now there is liv - ing faith.

(Verse 2 only)

out of the grip of dark - ness in - to the light of grace. Just like Laz - a - rus,
All of my hope and free - dom I found in Je - sus' name. Just like Laz - a - rus,

1 **2**

oh, You brought me back to life. (back) to life. No long - er
oh, You brought me back

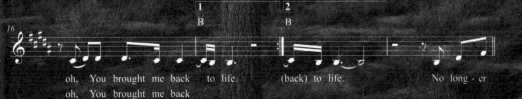

HOMETOWN

14

I'm one of those guys with deep hometown pride. I was born and raised in San Diego County, and I still live here to this day. I may be biased, but it's my favorite place in the world. It's got beaches, and it's got mountains. It has cool metro areas and wide-open farmland. There's great coffee and great food (sushi and tacos anyone!?). The biking, hiking, running, and generally anything outdoors is incredible all year 'round. Don't even get me started on the sunsets over the ocean. They will blow your mind on a daily basis. AND THE WEATHER!! C'MON! Arguably the best in the world. Yes, the downside is the price. You could buy a mini-mansion in other places for what it would cost to buy a one bedroom shack by the beach here in San Diego. But my family and friends are here. My church community is here. The streets I learned how to drive on are here. It's home, and I love it. But even more than loving it, my wife Mallory and I have a real sense of calling from God to be here.

As you read this, I imagine pictures are popping up in your minds of the places significant to your story. Take a minute to look around you at the place that God has called you to in this season. Wherever you find yourself, I want to remind you that anywhere and everywhere is a backdrop for God's unfolding story. God's power, artistry, miracles, love, and grace are on the move all around you. It doesn't matter if you're in a dorm room, at your kitchen table, in a hospital bed, or on a vacation in Hawaii. When we see the world around us through the lens of the reality of a loving God, everything changes! And as we carry His spirit and love into the world, we become catalysts of holy change for the Kingdom of God.

Our heaven-filled presence turns coffee shops into cathedrals. Our homes become holy places as we gather in the name of Jesus. Sunsets aren't just sunsets anymore, they are reminders of His beauty and artistry. When we look at things with this Kingdom perspective, what we once thought of as mundane becomes rich with purpose, meaning, beauty, and intentionality.

I wrote this song "Hometown" not just out of a love for the place I live. I wrote it because I have been growing in the practice of trying to see God's presence everywhere. I ask questions like: God, where are You in this? What are You up to here? How can I come alongside Your plans and purposes for this moment? In Jesus, there are adventures to be had even in the smallest and sleepiest towns. God is on the move everywhere, and He has bestowed upon us the incredible gift of joining in it all with Him.

So, join me in the prayer of this song...

Awaken hearts, send revival, right here in my HOMETOWN

Key Questions:

1. Where have you seen God's faithfulness in your hometown? How has your own story seen God's redemptive hand at work?

2. How can you intentionally start praying for a move of God in your town or city? How might God be asking you to join Him in this work?

3. In what ordinary and common places in your life might God want you to start noticing His Kingdom coming and His Spirit moving?

Key Bible Verses to Meditate On:

Psalm 24:1 (CSB):
The earth and everything in it,
the world and its inhabitants,
belong to the Lord.

Matthew 6:9–10 (ESV):
"Our Father in heaven,
hallowed be your name.
Your kingdom come,
your will be done,
on earth as it is in heaven."

Galatians 5:25 (NIV):
Since we live by the Spirit, let us keep in step with the Spirit.

CREDITS

THIS IS OUR GOD
Phil Wickham, Steven Furtick, Brandon Lake, Pat Barrett

© 2023 Phil Wickham Music, Simply Global Songs (BMI), Music by Elevation Worship Publishing (BMI), Brandon Lake Music, Maverick City Publishing Worldwide (ASCAP) (admin at. essentialmusicpublishing. com), Housefires Sounds, Capitol CMG Genesis (ASCAP) (admin. at capitolcmgpublishing.com). All Rights Reserved. Used by permission.

I BELIEVE
Phil Wickham, Jonathan Smith, Chris Davenport

© 2023 Phil Wickham Music, Simply Global Songs (BMI), Cashagamble Jet Music, Be Essential Songs (BMI) (admin. at essentialmusicpublishing.com), CDavs Music, Songs For TIM (BMI) (admin. at capitolcmgpublishing.com). All Rights Reserved. Used by permission.

SUNDAY IS COMING
Phil Wickham, Steven Furtick, Jonathan Smith, Adrian Disch

© 2023 Phil Wickham Music, Simply Global Songs (BMI), Music by Elevation Worship Publishing (BMI), Cashagamble Jet Music, Be Essential Songs (BMI) (admin. at essentialmusicpublishing.com), Extraction Time Publishing (BMI). All Rights Reserved. Used by permission.

CREATOR
Phil Wickham, Bryan Fowler, Kristyn Getty

© 2023 Phil Wickham Music, Simply Global Songs (BMI), bryanfowlersongs, Be Essential Songs (BMI) (admin. at essentialmusicpublishing.com), Getty Music Publishing (BMI) (admin. at Music Services). All Rights Reserved. Used by permission.

PRAISE THE LORD
Phil Wickham, Mia Fieldes, Jonathan Smith, Brandon Lake, Steven Furtick

© 2023 Phil Wickham Music, Simply Global Songs (BMI), Upside Down Under, Be Essential Songs (BMI), Cashagamble Jet Music, Be Essential Songs (BMI), Brandon Lake Music, Maverick City Publishing Worldwide (ASCAP), Music by Elevation Worship Publishing (BMI) (admin. at essentialmusicpublishing. com). All Rights Reserved. Used by permission.

THE JESUS WAY
Phil Wickham, Jonathan Smith

© 2023 Phil Wickham Music, Simply Global Songs (BMI), Cashagamble Jet Music, Be Essential Songs (BMI) (admin. at essentialmusicpublishing.com). All Rights Reserved. Used by permission.

WAIT
Phil Wickham, Jacob Sooter, Ran Jackson, Chandan Bangar, Jane Williams

PSALM 23
Phil Wickham

ISN'T HE GOOD
Phil Wickham, Brandon Lake, Ricky Jackson, Steven Furtick

100%
Phil Wickham, Jonathan Smith, Evan Wickham

YOUR NAME IS HOLY
Phil Wickham, Jonathan Smith, Sean Curran, Brian Johnson

RELATIONSHIP
Phil Wickham, Brandon Lake, Steven Furtick

BACK TO LIFE
Phil Wickham, Chris Davenport, Reuben Morgan, Benjamin Fielding, Brian Johnson, Zahriya Zachary

HOMETOWN
Phil Wickham, Jacob Tynes, Benji Horning, Jen Horning

PRIVFC.US

STAY CONNECTED

LISTEN TO THE SONGS, SEE UPCOMING TOUR DATES, AND MORE AT

PHILWICKHAM.COM

MORE FROM PHIL WICKHAM

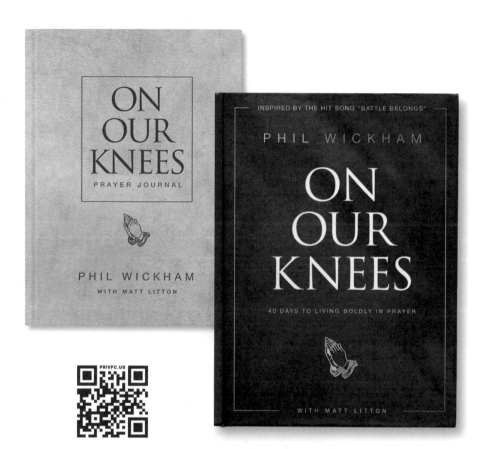

40 DAY TO LIVING **BOLDLY IN PRAYER**
INSPIRED BY THE HIT SONG "BATTLE BELONGS

AVAILABLE NOW AT
PHILWICKHAM.COM

LISTEN AS YOU READ

AVAILABLE NOW